DATE DUE

~~MY 29 97~~			
~~JY 3 '97~~			
~~JY 23 '97~~			
~~NO 2 5 '15~~			

DEMCO 38-296

SELECTED POEMS

by

SHU TING

— An Authorized Collection —

A Renditions Paperback

perbacks

ned by

for Translation

The Chinese University of Hong Kong

General Editor

Eva Hung

Printed in Hong Kong

Contents

Editor's Preface

The term Misty Poetry is synonymous with the first outburst of literary creativity in China's Post-Cultural Revolution era. Like the word "intellectual", *menglong* or Misty was initially used in denigration (1980), as a condemnation of a poetic style and voices which were a clear departure from the accepted poetic production of Socialist Realism in Communist China. However, almost as soon as the word was used, it gained popularity as a neutral label for the group of young poets whose work appeared in the underground literary magazine *Today* — the same group of poets which establishment figures tried to condemn. The Misty group consisted of five core members: Bei Dao, Yang Lian, Jiang He, Shu Ting and Gu Cheng. None of them accepted the classification of *menglong*, all stressed the stylistic diversity of the group. However, the label stuck. In 1985, the poetry magazine *Stars* (*Xingxing*) conducted a survey and published a list of the ten most popular contemporary poets in China, which included all the core members of the Misty group. In 1986, a national conference on contemporary poetry held in Lanzhou gave formal recognition to the influence — and thus the achievements — of the Misty poets. At the time of the writing of this preface, Bei Dao and Yang Lian are living in exile; Gu Cheng committed suicide in New Zealand in 1993, immediately after he killed his wife.

Of the five, Shu Ting is the only woman and the first to gain acceptance by the mainstream literary establishment. Her work was published as early as 1980 in the official poetry magazine *Shikan*. This is no doubt because she is perceived to be the least political among the five poets. However, in the context of Communist ideology which demanded the total subservience of literature to the needs of political propaganda, the deliberate exclusion of politics in literary creation can be interpreted as a highly political act. This is not to say that Shu Ting is a political writer — she would be the first to deny such a label. What one has to remember is the background to Shu Ting's early works. She started writing during the Cultural Revolution (1966-1976) when every aspect of ordinary life in China was politicized and the expression of individual feelings was highly dangerous. In such a stifling atmosphere, the directness and simplicity of Shu Ting's poetry, with its focus on individual emotions, caused a considerable stir. Her voice is distinctly feminine, but not feminist. In the decade after the Cultural Revolution, when China was struggling to recover from ten years of trauma, Shu Ting's gentle poetic voice and her faith in the human spirit drew a remarkably large following. Her aspirations are best summed up in the following untitled poem:

> People, please understand me.
>
> I do not consider myself a poet; I know I will never be a thinker (however willing I am). Yet I am deeply conscious of the fact that, today, people have an urgent need for respect, trust and love. I want to try my best to show my concern for my fellow human beings.
>
> Barriers must be cleared away, masks taken off. I believe that people can understand each other because it *is* possible to find the way to our hearts. (1980)

The style of Shu Ting's writing changed around late 1985 to 1986, when she experimented on the one hand with modernist imagery, and on the other hand with a deliberately unpolished style. "The Archae-opteryx" (p. 99) is representative of the former while "goodbye, white handkerchief" (p. 108) is the best example of the latter. Despite such changes, her poetic voice remains recognizable and distinctly femi-nine.

Throughout the 1980s Shu Ting was arguably the most popular poet with the Chinese reading public. Her first poetry collection, *A Boat with Two Masts*, was published in 1980. Subsequent collections include

Selected Lyrical Poems of Shu Ting & Gu Cheng (1981), *The Singing Iris* (1986) and *The Archaeopteryx* (1992). She has also published two prose collections since 1990. This Renditions Paperback is the first collection of her work in English translation. The forty-nine poems collected herein (including two poem cycles) cover Shu Ting's entire poetic career — from the mid 1970s to the early 1990s.

Shu Ting, real name Gong Peiyu 龔珮瑜 (Gong Shuting 龔舒婷 was the name she used at school), was born in 1952 in Jinjiang, Fujian province, and grew up in Gulangyu, an island unique for its western-influenced architecture dating back to the early Republican period, and for its proximity to Taiwan. Her parents were both from a middle-class intellectual background and as a result suffered considerable hardship in the various political campaigns leading up to the Cultural Revolution. This led eventually to their separation, and Shu Ting was brought up in the house of her loving maternal grandmother. The experience of these formative years was one of the dominant emotional influences in her life, crystallizing in some of her best poems — "Curriculum Vitae" (p. 119) and "A Letter to Second Uncle" (p. 121).

During the Cultural Revolution Shu Ting, like other young people of her generation, was sent down to work in the poverty-stricken countryside before she finished her secondary education. She was allowed to return to the city of Xiamen in Fujian in 1973, where, as a "young person awaiting employment", she was assigned to menial jobs at construction sites, and later in steel and textile factories. Both her experiences in the countryside and as a factory hand have found expression in some of her early poems collected here. In the late 1980s she was accepted as a full-time writer by the official Fujian Writers Association, giving her the salary of a government-supported writer. She was one of the last Chinese writers to be accorded such financial support — the practice has now been discontinued.

Despite her international reputation, Shu Ting remains something of a literary recluse. It was not until 1989 that she started accepting invitations to attend literary events overseas — as a means of

meeting long absent friends. For almost twenty years Shu Ting had also
resisted all attempts by major Chinese newspapers and television to
interview her. Her identity as China's leading woman poet was com-
pletely unknown to her neighbours on idyllic Gulangyu until late 1992.

Shu Ting is married to Chen Zhongyi, a literary critic and college
teacher. They have one son.

The idea for this book first came from Henry Y.H. Zhao. With
Shu Ting's consent, some of the translations in manuscript form,
together with the responsibility of editing the book, were handed over
to me in 1989. Contrary to the opinion of some critics (including Shu
Ting's husband, Chen), I think that her lyrics of the late 1980s possess
a stylistic purity and an emotional maturity which far surpass her earlier
works. This volume presents a balanced sample of Shu Ting's *oeuvre* up
to 1990, as well as Chen's and her own views on her poetry, which
will provide readers with a broader perspective of the various forces
which shape a poet's work. I am grateful to Shu Ting and Chen
Zhongyi for the time they spent with me in Hong Kong discussing the
poems considered for this collection, and to the translators for their
enthusiasm and support.

Eva Hung
July 1994
Chinese University of Hong Kong

A Dialogue with Shu Ting and Chen Zhongyi

Q: To your mind, what is the difference between an ordinary woman and a woman poet?

Shu Ting: I *am* an ordinary woman. I don't think there is any difference between the two, but of course society looks at them differently. Women poets are often expected to sacrifice many aspects of themselves as ordinary women. Yet because of the woman poet's social relationships, she has to play other roles. For example my husband wants me to be a good mother, a good wife, and a good daughter-in-law. And yet at the same time because he is a literary critic he wants me to write. It is rather contradictory sometimes. I find it impossible to prepare a meal and write poetry simultaneously.

I normally write at night, after my son has gone to bed. Every time I write, the emotions are so intense I cannot sleep for the rest of the night. And yet I have to get up the next day at 6:30 to make breakfast and get my son ready for school. So there are conflicts.

Yet I realize that if I were just a working woman with fixed office hours — a nurse, a driver, or a teacher — I'd still be taking care of the family after work. In that sense there is little difference between me and any other working woman in China. The real difference is that they can forget about their work once they leave their work place, but because my work involves the emotions, it is not possible for me to say "Now I'm off duty"; you cannot just draw the line.

When I was a factory worker I could refuse to work overtime. After I came off the assembly line I was my own woman. Now my thoughts and emotions are inextricably linked with my family, which is why writing poetry has become very difficult for me. But I'm always telling myself that my problems are not unique — I am just an ordinary woman.

There is of course a basic difference between an ordinary woman and a woman poet; it is the latter's sensitivity to language. It is the same kind of difference which distinguishes an ordinary man from a male writer. It is my firm belief that what makes a poet is her command of the language. For me, writing poetry is not a matter of expressing my feelings, it is having the words to express them.

Q to Chen: You are Shu Ting's husband; you are also a literary critic. How is Shu Ting the woman and Shu Ting the poet different now from the person you knew ten years ago? The watersheds must have been marriage and motherhood.

Chen: There are tremendous differences. In terms of quantity and quality as a poet, I think that she is over her peak. I have a personal bias: I think that women poets and lyrical poets last a decade or so. There was a time when I urged her to write, but then I came to the realization that perhaps poets and ballerinas are similar in one sense: they cannot go on forever.

She stopped writing for three years after we got married. Having a child is probably a very traumatic experience for a woman, and besides she had to adjust emotionally to family life. I think that some of her post-85 poems such as "Colours" and "... in between" belong to her early period — a mixture of classical and post-romantic feelings with modernist techniques. Those are my favourite poems.

Q: Your husband seems to like your earlier works the best. Do you agree with him?

Shu Ting: I don't really like them. Last year [1992] in New York I had to give a public reading of some of my poems, and almost all the poems which had been translated into English were pre-1985 ones, with some going back to the early 70s. After reading some of them aloud, I simply could not go on. It was too embarrassing. I felt like a mature woman made to wear little girls' clothes.

However, I think there is a difference between me and male authors. Men tend to plan ahead when they write, and they literally glow when they reread their more successful works; while I just write and then forget about my poems — I have yet to reread anything in my poetry collections. I simply dare not look back at my own career, so I can't talk about likes and dislikes.

I never plan before I write, and can never be forced to write. There was a time when my husband kept urging me to "look for inspiration", and I ended up not writing anything for a year. I can never write on assignment either, not even prose pieces.

Q: Can you tell me why you feel so indifferent towards your early poems when they clearly have a strong appeal to readers?

Shu Ting: Well, I have always been true to myself in my writing, so that may account for reader appeal. The fact is I never write for the sake of publication. It's always the publishers and editors who come and ask for my work. My early poems — such as "To an Oak" (1977), written in a personal letter to a friend — were not written with publication in mind; at that time [during the Cultural Revolution] publication was impossible. The feelings behind the poems were simple and personal. And then when they were published, people talked incessantly about them, so much so that I became rather annoyed. There was also intense criticism of me and my work. I was accused of free love, of using people emotionally — that was before I got married and society still subscribed to feudal values. I had a terrible time because I was entirely unprepared for any of this. I was still working at the factory and I couldn't bear the way my co-workers looked at me. Imagine you have something which you hold precious, and a lot of people come and touch it with their dirty hands — that is how I feel about my early poems; I can't bear to reread them because of this.

Chen: Shu Ting is different from most other poets in that her early poems were all written for specific individuals; they were private thoughts. She did not publish anything until 1979. To have something extremely private in the hands of the public — especially when the outlook of that public was so different from hers — that probably accounts for her ambivalence towards these works.

Q: Talking about early poetry, what do you think of the works of the earlier generations of Chinese poets — those writing between the twenties and the forties?

Shu Ting: I can see that I'm falling into my own trap. I prefer the early poetry of writers of the twenties and thirties — the early works of poets such as Wen Yiduo, He Qifang and Ai Qing. This is also true of the works of poets of my generation. The only exception is Cai Qijiao, my mentor. I feel that his recent poems are far superior to his early works, both in terms of simplicity of language and of feeling. However, the poets may feel differently — I think that Bei Dao, like me, would in all likelihood say that his preference is *not* for his early poems.

Q: I understand that you are now writing more prose pieces than poetry. What is the difference between the two?

Shu Ting: To me — and I do not know whether it is the same for other people — prose is easier than poetry in the sense that it is emotionally less demanding. In the few days from the building-up to a poem until after it is finished, I am in a feverish state, losing interest in everything around me. That is why sometimes I avoid poetry out of fear of this feverish feeling. As soon as I feel that a poem might be in the making, I pick up a book, or go and see a film, hoping the inspiration will go away. But there comes a point when poetry catches up with me, and I have to write because there is no escaping it. Writing prose for me is much more relaxing emotionally. I have a feeling that I will concentrate on poetry again some time in the future, but at the moment I am taking a break.

Q: It seems that you have always avoided talking about your own poetry. Why?

Shu Ting: A poet cannot really talk about her own poetry. I think that if she can talk clearly and systematically about the ideas and feelings she tries to express in her poems, than those poems would never have been written. I do not think I am unique in this — it must be true of poets like Gu Cheng and Bei Dao as well.

6 September 1993
transcribed, translated and edited by Eva Hung

Gifts

My dream is the dream that the pond has
Whose existence is not merely to reflect the sky
But to let the surrounding willows and ferns
Suck me dry.
Through the tree roots I'll enter the veins of their leaves
Yet withering brings no sorrow to me
For I shall have expressed myself
And gained life.

My happiness is the happiness of sunlight
In a brief moment I leave behind everlasting works
In the pupils of children's eyes
Kindling sparks of gold.
In the sprouting of seedlings
I sing an emerald green song.
I am simple but abundant
So I am deep.

My grief is the grief of seasonal birds
Only Spring understands such strong love
Suffering all kinds of hardships and failure
To fly into a future of warmth and light.
Oh the bleeding wings
Will write a line of heartfelt verse
To penetrate all souls
And enter all times.

All that I feel
Is the gift of the earth.

A Boat with Two Masts

Fog has drenched my two wings
But the wind will not allow me to dally
Oh land, land that I love
Only yesterday I said goodbye to you
Today you are here again
Tomorrow we will
Meet again at a different latitude

It was a storm, a lamp
That held us together
It was another storm, another lamp
That parted us to the east and west
Even to the edge of the sky and the farthest shore
Surely every morning and evening
You will be on my route
I will be in your sight

Goodbye in the Rain

I really wanted to wrench open the door and rush towards you,
And cry my heart out on your ample shoulders.
"I cannot bear it, I really cannot bear it."

I really wanted to take your hand,
And run away to the freshly cleared sky and open fields,
Without shrinking or looking back.

I really wanted to gather all my tenderness,
In my eyes that have no power of speech,
And make you at last realize.

I really wanted to, really wanted to,
My pain changes to grief,
Never-ending in thought, inexpressible in words.

A Boat

A small boat
For whatever reason
Lies marooned on its side on
A desolate stony bank
The paint has not quite gone
But the mast is already broken
There are no green trees to give shade
Or grass willing to grow

The sea at high tide
Is only a few yards away
The waves sigh
Water birds anxiously flap their wings
Though the endless ocean
Has domains far away
In this vicinity
It has lost its last strength

Across that eternal divide
Lost, they gaze at each other
Love crosses the boundary of life and death
And the vacancy of hundreds of years
Weaves a cross pattern of glances, ancient and yet always fresh
Surely deeply felt love
Does not decay along with the boards of the boat
Surely the fluttering soul
Will not be imprisoned for ever on the threshold of freedom

When You Walk Beneath My Window

When you walk beneath my window
bless me, please,
because the light is burning.

The light is burning —
against the darkness of night,
like the weaving light of a fishing-boat.
Imagine my little house
like a little boat pushed ahead of a storm,
not yet sunk
because you can still see a light.

The light is burning —
and the curtain presents my shadow
as if I were instead an aged man
without strong and open gestures,
ever more hunched over,
though my heart is not at all senile.
See, my light is still burning.

The light is burning —
possessed by a love like fire
and ready to give back greetings to each and all.
The light is burning —
its fuel is a kind of dignified arrogance, indeed,
surveying any and all oppressions, open or hidden.
And when does this light burn most brightly?
When you begin to understand me.

Because my light is burning still now,
bless me, please,
you, walking beneath my window.

19 April 1976

To an Oak

If I love you —
I won't be like the trumpet creeper
Flaunting itself on your tall branches,
If I love you —
I won't be like the lovesick bird,
Repeating to the green shade its monotonous song;
Nor like a brook,
Bringing cool solace the year round;
Nor like a perilous peak,
Adding to your height, complementing your grandeur;
Nor even sunlight,
Nor even spring rain.
No, these are not enough!
I must be a kapok tree by your side;
Standing by you as a tree,
Our roots clasped underground,
Our leaves touching in the clouds.

With every breeze
We salute each other,
But no one
Will understand our language.
You have your trunk of steel and iron branches,
Like knives, like swords,
Like spears.
I have my huge, red flowers,
Like heavy sighs,
Like valiant torches.
We share the burdens of cold, storms, lightning;
We share the joys of mists, vapours, rainbows.
We may seem forever severed,
But arc lifelong companions.
This is the greatest love;
This is constancy:
Love —
I love not just your robust form,
I love the ground you hold, the earth you stand on.

27 March 1977

Longing

A colourful wall chart without contours
A pure, insoluble equation
A zither stirring the rosaries of raindrops hanging from the eaves
A pair of oars that will never reach the far shore

Waiting silently, like flower buds
Gazing from afar, like the setting sun
Perhaps an ocean is hidden within
But out flow only two teardrops

Oh, in a distant corner of my heart
in the recesses of my soul

May 1978

Two, Maybe Three Different Memories

The wine cup fallen,
a stone path floats in the moonlight;
where grasses were beaten down
an azalea has been dropped and abandoned.

Eucalyptus trees begin to turn,
stars turning together — a kaleidoscope;
beyond a rusted iron anchor,
the spinning sky is caught in my eyes.

I place my book to block the candle-light,
I touch my finger lightly to my teeth;
in a fragile peace the evening finds me
alive dreaming, half in shadows, half awake.

23 May 1978

a roadside encounter

the phoenix tree suddenly tilts
the bicycle bell's ring hangs in air
earth swiftly reverses its rotation
back to that night ten years ago

the phoenix tree gently sways again
the ringing bell sprinkles floral fragrance along the
        trembling street
darkness gathers, then seeps away
the dawning light of memory merges with the light in your eyes

maybe this didn't happen
just an illusion spawned by a familiar road
even if this did happen
I'm used to not shedding any tears

March 1979

Perhaps
— To an author in isolation

Perhaps what we can think to say
    will never have readers.
Perhaps our journey was already wrong in the beginning,
    and therefore ends wrong, too.
Perhaps the lamps we light one by one
    are blown out by the winds one by one.
Perhaps we shall have exerted ourselves to the utmost to light
    the darkness
    and have no fire extra to keep ourselves warm.

Perhaps the tears we wept till we couldn't
    did make the land more fertile.
Perhaps the sun we sang into being
    also sings us to life.
Perhaps the more weight on our shoulders,
    the grander the faith we had.
Perhaps we cried out vigorously on the sufferings of others
    but had to be still on our own misfortunes.

Perhaps
ours was a call that wouldn't be resisted;
we had (and have) no other choice.

December 1979

A Late Autumn Evening in Beijing

1

Night spills over the cordon of street lamps
to extinguish the stars
Wind follows in its wake, shaking every poplar tree
whipping up tides of noise

Let us go too
and fight for the sky
or be a small leaf
echoing the songs of the forest

2

I am not afraid of appearing weak before you
Let the ranks of high speed cars
destroy the dignity of the city
In the world behind your shoulders
a slit of a haven

In the night pierced by headlights
on the orange red horizon
we are alone
But there is my flimsy shadow
standing beside you

3

When you are just you
and I am just me
we quarrel
and we make peace
a pair of weird friends

When you are no longer you
and I am no longer me
between our joined arms
there is no welding line
nor the slightest gap

4

If it weren't for you
If it weren't for the strange city
        the drizzle, the fallen leaves, the footsteps

If there is no need for explanation
If there is no need for protection
        road signs, the zebra, traffic batons

If there is no meeting
If the meeting can be forgotten
        silence, shadows

5

I can feel it: this moment
is vanishing slowly
into part of the past
into memory
Your flickering smile
floats
in layers of tears

I can feel it: tonight and tomorrow night
are separated by a long life
Our hearts have to trudge through too many years
before their meeting on the other side of the world
I want to beg you
to pause for a while. Under the street lamp
I looked away in silence

6

Night closes behind you
You are heading toward the starry sky
to become a riddle without key
An ice-cold drop of tear
hanging on the face of "eternity"
is hiding in the remnants of my dream

December 1979

Assembly Line

On the assembly line of Time
Nights huddle together
We come down from the factory assembly lines
And join the assembly line going home
Overhead
An assembly line of stars trails across the sky
By our side
A young tree looks dazed on its assembly line

The stars must be tired
Thousands of years have passed
Their journey never changes
The young trees are ill
Dust and monotony deprive them
Of grain and colour
I can feel it all
Because we beat to the same rhythm

Yet strangely
The only thing I do not feel
Is my own existence
As though the woods and stars
Maybe out of habit
Maybe out of sorrow
No longer have the strength to care
About a destiny they cannot alter

Jan.-Feb. 1980

Fallen Leaf

1

A sliver of a moon, like a piece of thin ice,
floats on the cool light of evening.
You send me home, and on the way
we find ourselves sighing quietly,
not because we are sad.
We can't say why:
the leaves falling in the pull of the wind
pass on to us
a kind of mood.
Only after our goodbye
do I hear your footsteps
mingled with the fallen leaves.

2

When Spring is everywhere
whispering in our ears,
but the fallen leaves underfoot suggest
the last of the winter guilt and darkened memories,
shaking us deeply
and making our eyes avoid meeting,
all the more
our thoughts are one once again.

Seasons are only for trees,
leaving annual rings.
Poems about fallen leaves and buds
come out by the thousands of lines.
But a tree can have
only one eternal theme:
"The free extension of oneself into sky,
never leaving the earth."

3

Outside the windows and door, the wind
brings me news of you,
tells me you are walking beneath a kapok tree
shaking down a rain of flowers,
tells me it is chilly on a Spring evening
but there is no chill in your heart.

Suddenly I feel I am a fallen leaf, too,
lying on the dark earth.
The wind might be a dirge for me.
I wait peacefully
for the green dream
to gleam once again in my body.

May 1980

homeward bound

the wind tonight
seems full of echoes
wind in the pines, fireflies, lamplight from a hydroelectric
     station
all reminding me of a distant dream
my memory is like a small overloaded wooden bridge
spanning the banks of time
does moonlight still scamper merrily down the steps on the
     other side?
my heart trembles, fearful of starting the journey

don't think back, don't think back
my wandering feet are tired
I rest my head on the shoulder of the mountain
I seem to have walked a long, long way
yet I'm back where I started
innocent eyes rise again like the stars
shining on me, just as ten years ago
maybe if I hold out my hands
a golden apple will fall
a waterfall of blood
brightens my soul as though it's in flames

this can't be true, can't be true
youth has turned its back and walks through a dense forest of
     cries
toward oblivion

A Love Song for this Land

I love this land, like
I love my taciturn father

Oh this land warmed by tides of hot blood
Oh this land greased by fermenting sweat
Palpitating under the weight of ploughs and bare feet
Driven by the immense heat at its heart
        rising and sinking
Shouldering statues, monuments, museums
Yet writing its last judgement on fault planes
Mine
Oh frozen, muddy, parched land
Mine
Oh wrathful, magnanimous, relentless land
Land that gives me my complexion and my tongue
Land that gives me my wisdom and my strength

I love this land, like
I love my gentle solicitous mother

Oh plentiful land covered with the sun's kisses
Oh generous land wasting her flow of milk
Taking in layer upon layer of fallen leaves
Sprouting crop after crop of green shoots
Discarded over and over
But never unfaithful
Creating sounds, colours, patterns
Though everyone calls you dirt and mud
Mine
Oh pitch black, blood drenched, glimmering white land
Mine
Oh luxuriant, lonely, frustrated land
Land that gives me my love and my hatred
Land that gives me my pain and my joy

My father endowed me with a boundless dream
My mother a heart sensitive and true
My poems are
        the ever yearning necklace trees
Pouring out day and night
        my ever constant love for this land

October 1980

brother, I'm here

the night is cool like the evening tide
rising up each uneven step of the stairs
invading your heart
you sit on the threshold
the small, dark house, mouth gaping
squats behind you
the scholartree shakes, leaves flutter down like birds in flight
on waves pale as moonlight
tiny gold coins float

you pertain to the sun
to prairies, embankments, eyes of black jade
you pertain to snowstorms
to roads, torches, hands extended to help
you are a warrior
your life resounds
like a bell
shattering the shadows in man's heart

the wind absconds in unfamiliar footsteps
won't believe
you're still grieving

but, brother
I'm here
coming to you from your thoughts
a news-stand, a bench, apple seeds
resurrected in the warmth of your memory
leaving behind smiles and lights
leaving behind a light-hearted rhythm
leaving

along the squares of a piece of manuscript paper

as long as there is wind at night
wind changes the direction of our thoughts
as long as your trumpet suddenly falls silent
seeking harmony
I will be back
by your side calmly saying
brother, I'm here

May 1981

Evening Star

1

Rising from the galloping cloud of red horses
    you blue and calm
    blue, and calm
as if to bid farewell
    to say the last words
your quick glance
    is full of love

You undo, one by one, the arms
    of the hawthorn tree
    that urge you to stay
and sink into the abyss of night
I still stand where you once shone
my thought flying in the sunset glow
    together with the late birds
— till the moon is on top of the pine trees
This I promise: even without you by my side
I shall grope my way upwards
    never say tired
    never say tired
A thousand times I'll offer
a heart as pure as yours

2

This is my city
I am waiting for your arrival

Chimneys, cables, fishbone antennas
cast a net over the depleted sky
Wild swans and larks have all been warned
In their sketch-books the kids have only
wheatears, guns and a moon drawn by compass
so they have to dream all night

This is the evening of my city
and I believe that you will arrive

The sun slips away along the foot of the wall
The dark clock tower and painted new blocks
look like stage sets
The sea lies silently by the rocks
the wind stands silently by the palm trees
this is only a short pause in the song

My city has so many windows opening to you
My city has so many eyes looking toward you
the pot flowers on the balcony
the kites that scamper on the roof
even that tuneless
violin in the garret
Over everyone's head, in everyone's heart
there is a star belonging to herself

This is why I believe you are coming
This is why I am sure you have come

15 July 1981

Evening Montage

1

The sun is spread thin over the low wall,
This summer is as cold as ever.

2

The tearful mezzo-soprano
is trying to melt the evening
into a pool of syrup

May all gummed up wings
fly away, quivering.

3

Flowers that have once withered
know all about spring;
Those that have never bloomed
are the first to imagine withering.

4

The masson pine tree begs the wind
to let him be his old self.
The wind goes on mocking him.
The tree is enraged
— but he can't stop swaying.

5

The birds that flew out to sing at daybreak
have yet to return.
The small wood in the loneliness of the dusk
hangs like a curtain of melancholy.

6

I must have made a pact with the evening.
Often she stops at my window
expectantly.
What should I give her? Who is it meant for?
this is a secret
I no longer remember

She shakes her head,
and walks away.

7

Wandering shadow, oh
are you reaching out with your tentacles again?

8

and there is no gunshot.

9

This world is destined to lie open
like a hand of cards.
Why should it
put on such a haughty look
scaring everyone to death.

10

Banks of shadows at the foot of the buildings
Are bewildered
By their own lights.

11

Gurgling water
reminds us of mustard flowers, banks of streams,
and bronzed peasant girls.
But it is actually people coming off work
talking about the price of fish
around the public stand-pipe.

12

Moonlight winds itself round the soft branches of the palm trees
only to set them free;
The stars bounced into the grass
crawl out, chuckling.

When footsteps foretell someone's approach
all sunflowers stop their hide-and-seek.
Someone says, I think I heard something.
The wind muffling its mouth says
I'm not surprised.

13

The luggage is ready
but the bell on the platform doesn't ring.

We are destined never to arrive
at where we want to go.

14

I cry when I want to cry,
but they teach me to smile;
I smile when I want to smile,
but they teach me to cry.

They are right.
I am right too.

15

The thoughts jabbering in the chicken coop,
how far can they soar
    when they are let loose?

16

Faces behind the lattice window;
Souls behind the eyes;
Primeval forest behind the souls;
the myna birds in the wood
have learned to be quiet.

17

In the night some things must light up.
Those that do
people call them stars.

August-October 1981

The Singing Iris

— your light has raised a pale halo above my sorrow

1

In your embrace
I've become a singing iris
Your breath a soft breeze that stirs me
beneath the light of a jangling moon

Take your broad palm
and cover me
for now

2

Can I dream
Snow. Vast forest
ancient wind chimes and leaning pagoda
Can I have a real Christmas tree
hung with
ice skates, magic flutes and fairy tales
blazing, shooting sparks of happiness
Can I run laughing through the streets

3

What of my little basket
the grass harvest from my high-yield plot
my old water jug
and parched lunch break beneath my scaffolding
the butterfly bow I never had
my English exercises: I love you, love you
my shadow in the streetlamp light — accordioned, stretched out
What of my tears — poured out, blinked back
        times without number

There's more
There's more

In my dreams I turn away slightly
Don't ask me why
Memories chirr like crickets hiding in the corners
Low but persistent

4

Let me dream peacefully
Don't leave me
On that short short street
we've walked long months into years

Let me dream undisturbed
Don't startle me
Ignore that circling flock of crows
but let no dark clouds shadow your eyes

Let me dream foolishly
Don't laugh at me
I want to go fresh each day into your verses
returning each night flushed to your side

Let me dream with abandon
forgive, even tolerate my domineering ways
When I say: You're mine, mine!
Love, don't blame me ...
I crave
        the millions of billowing waves, surging zeal
        swallowing you up a million times

5

Heads together,
we catch the express train to the moon
Then the world falls whistling away behind
Time spins madly
        rolling down all around like an avalanche

We gaze at each other in silence
souls like a field in a painting on display
Then eddies of sunshine
entice us deeper into
        stillness, fulfilment, harmony

6

And so
we sit holding hands in the dark
letting a voice, ancient yet young,
resound through our hearts
And should a king come knocking
you needn't pay him any mind

Still ...

7

Wait — What was that? What sound
awakens the scarlet metre in my veins
        oh sea ever-waking
        while I'm light-headed
What's that? Whose will is it
opens wide the eyes of my flesh, my spirit
        "You must take up your cross each day
and follow me"

8

Umbrella-like dream
flutters away like dandelion floss
ringed mountains all around

9

Oh triangular plum blossoms of my emotions
you'd rather wither and die
returning to your rainswept hillside
not reel and sway here in the vase

Oh wild swans of my nature
though you sustain bullet wounds
still you soar across the unobstructed winter sky
not pining for the balustraded spring

Yet my name and my convictions
have entered the race together
running for the people's personal best
I have no right to a break
In the sprint of life
there is no finish, only dash speed

10

To the sky,
highest ruling body, I
lift my face

Ah wind, you can take me
But my heart is still my own
recognizing the right to be unhappy

11

Love, lift your lamp
light my way
Let me be scattered far and wide with my poems
the bell of ideals strikes beyond the marshland, so gentle the
        night
villages and towns cluster in the circle of my arms, let lamplight
nudge my poems along as I trudge on my way
the road brandishes its tentacles and shouts: you shall not pass
but the land streams criss-cross has given road signs to flowers

12

I walk the iron grid of city streets toward the square
I walk into the pumpkin shed, out of the barley fields, deep into
    the wilderness
Life recasts me endlessly
a heavy yoke on one side and on the other a coronet of flowers
And no one knows —
I'm still your silly little girl who can't get her sums right
No matter how the symphony of the times drowns it
you'll still pick out my voice like no other

13

I stand very straight
fearless, proud, terribly young
buffets of agony in my heart
the sun at my temples
my yellow skin shining, translucent
my black hair profuse, luxuriant

Oh China my mother
your child answers to your voice
give her a new name

14

Call me your "birch sapling"
your "little star of blue", Mamma —
if the bullets come
let them find me first
smiling, eyes uncommonly bright
I slide slowly down from mother's shoulder
Don't cry you flowers and plants
the blood will catch fire on your billowing tips

....

15

When the time comes, my love
don't be sad
though there's no one now
        to raise her pale skirts
        through the lanes where cicadas chirr like rain
        coming to knock on your coloured-glass window

though there's no mischievous hand
    to set the alarm clock
    to angrily announce: everyone in his place now
    go on, get back on course
Don't scrawl a rough image of me
on a jade pedestal
Don't flip back through the calendar page by page
in the company of your solitary guitar

16

Your place
is under that flag
ideals make suffering glorious
this I entrust to the olive tree
the last words
I leave you

Come with the dove to find me
come in the morning
you'll find me in the love of the people
there you'll find
                    your singing iris

28 October 1981

Ah Min in the Café

Red light. Green light. Horns and bike bells
come through the French window
and set your immobile face
fiercely ablaze
All the noise
dimly illumines
the unfathomable silence
in your eyes
The cup brimful of night
is without any warmth

The clanging of the old tower bells
dully stretches and slackens
measurable and immeasurable distance
The ravens of time
carry away a woman in flocks
an unknown crisis
gathers all the feathery shadows
        along the path of memory
Reason doubts itself as it consoles the heart
that all this will pass

Pain and loneliness
can be the theme for one night
But is there a night
that belongs to you
The wantonly blazing lamps and cold stares
cast your reservation
into an ice sculpture
The soul and the name eager to escape
can't find a shadow to hide behind

The next day
the sun shines in plainsong. All this
has slowly turned into
a pop song

6 March 1984

In Memory of My Late Grandmother

Some memories are written on forms
    detailing deceased family members
Some memories are traced out in red
    once a year, and then fade
Some memories are loud spoken
    as though boasting an inheritance
Some memories have turned into folklore
    you tell the children, about grandma, years ago

Some memories are just misty eyes
    re-enacting the past through photographs
Some memories are silent
    like birds singing deep in the summer woods
Some memories are hidden paths
    where you linger, where you repent
Some memories are the tastes of life —
    that's grandpa, and he died soon after she was gone

Oh, thank god
those whom we miss
are now far removed from all this

5 May 1984

The names of the deceased are written in red on traditional Chinese tombstones.

Resurrection

staring through the mask
with eyes unfocused
he turns life into masquerade, but who is he
you laugh and you cackle, you wail and you weep
even the tiny spiral shell makes a sucking noise clinging to
the storm
yet he stays silent in all the din, but who is he

don't turn round
behind you there's only the ponderous universe

perhaps being is only an unceasing wave motion
that twins your whole body into a river
then, your double in looks but not in soul
stands on the bank, but who is he
the thing that cycles you from soil to sky
like a tree
from germination to decay
is it just water?

you don't have to listen hard
you can't examine in your hands
a flow chart to explain the sound of rain

and so the silkworm wriggles
through
one trap after another laid by itself
to arrive at a momentary eclosion
        to die
                on the wing

the Arthur who ascends the cross
comes down as Jesus, but
only once in two thousand years

December 1984

Twelve Nights of the Milky Way (TV Poetry)

Editor's Note

This long poem was conceived as an experiment in presenting poetry on television. Shu Ting, therefore, had specific visual images in mind when she wrote the twelve sections of the poem. As a result, this is perhaps the most cinematic of her works. Unfortunately, the experiment did not go beyond the script stage, and was never shown on television.

Shu Ting takes the story of two lovers separated by the Cultural Revolution as a basis for exploring the many external forces which shape our lives and loves. Though the setting of the Cultural Revolution when educated youths were sent down to live and work in China's poverty-stricken rural areas may be unfamiliar to some readers, the clash of loyalties and the force of objective circumstances experienced by the lovers are universal.

Though Shu Ting does not normally make a point of using literary allusions, such allusions are not at all rare in her poetry. The allusions she uses are generally of the kind which have passed from literature into the popular metaphoric vocabulary readily recognized and understood by the majority of Chinese readers. The "Milky Way" in the title of this long poem is one such case. It is an allusion to the tragic romance between the Cowherd and the Weaving Girl (the constellations Altair and Vega). The lovers are separated by the Milky Way and are only allowed to meet one night a year — the night of the seventh day of the seventh lunar month. This is a popular subject in Tang and Song poetry.

Another prominent literary allusion is the *yan*, or goose, a messenger bird. Most references to geese in classical poetry are lamentations that they do not carry any news from loved ones. Geese feature in a number of Shu Ting's poems.

The title of the last section of this long poem is one of the most famous lines of Tang-dynasty poetry. Chang E, a highly celebrated folkloric figure, stole her husband's Elixir for Immortality and ascended to the moon. The Tang romantic poet Li Shangyin (813?-858?) wrote what is arguably the most famous poem on Chang E, in which she is envisaged as living a life of loneliness in her heavenly abode and regretting having become immortal.

1. First Date

spring 1969
she
southern China   a ruin in a park

Tearful lamplight
Too weak to push the encircling darkness away
I held on to the magnolia tree, stubbornly
waiting for your reply
        cold moss on the stone statue penetrated me
        surrounded me
You said: I'm going back home to the north-west tomorrow
our path
divides here
I shook my head
no, that is not what you want to say
You sighed
backed away and looked at me
across an invisible iron fence
Why, why
tell me
....

The remains of a wall erected a shadow
A collapsing galaxy pressed down on me
I turned and ran away, someone
pulled at me from behind
I tugged at my skirt in anger, to find
it was caught in the fence

You bent down quickly
untangled my torn skirt
I battled with my tears
seeing, vaguely, a few petals
stuck
on your cloud-like black hair
All of a sudden your head
    sank
        and sank
On my bare foot green by grass
a soft kiss

2. A Message

same day
he
by the red mansion

On the curtains your profile
    was a warm marble statue
Under the grapetrellis I had drawn
    blood from my lips
Night
flowed by quietly

Your chin resting on your hand, like a blossom
    hanging from a tender stalk, deep in thought
Your hands fluttering on my chest
    like two pigeons flapping their wings
I closed my eyes
oh, memories ....

The wind   the snow   the emaciated path
    the run-down temple father once garrisoned
Eroding soil, longing eyes
    all calling out to their child
I'm coming
and yet —

Farewell, my southern flower
    too fragile for Siberian exile
Farewell, my very first poem
    beautiful but unreal
I walked away without looking back
as morning dew moistened the winding lane

3. A Letter

1971
she
countryside in western Fujian

Now I can swim across the torrents
and climb up the red-and-white lighthouse
Do you know that, my dear
Now I can walk alone in the forest at night
and then go home in a thunderstorm
Do you know that, my dear

I journey down your favourite books
and till every word you have uttered
I threw away my glass slippers
to walk on mountain paths like blood-vessels
carrying your old guitar laden with your fingerprints
Do you know that, my dear

My songs of anguish
have moved the mountains and clouds near and far
but my happiness — too shy and proud
has yet to germinate
Standing in front of an open window
I pray: oh wind oh wind

Do you know that, my dear

4. Diary (1)

1969-1975
he
north-western China

1. Plateau. Completely exposed
One solitary young tree
        struggling against the wind and sand
The earth sucks dry
two lines of sweaty footprints

                          the sun
                          is dying

2. From the rioting peasants' guns
rose
a morning star of hope
yet it has failed to mature into a never-setting sun

Thirty years of revolution
still standing on
a stone lion half buried in the earth?

3. And so we begin with *The Communist Manifesto*
we
begin with loneliness
until the exhausted halo of the oil lamp
blends completely
with the silver dawn on the window sill

4. My dream is a spring pond
your face, half sad, half glad
        crumples in the ripples
A whistle blows outside
the morning roll-call

5. Diary (2)

1975-1977
he
north-western China

1. She walked in, dusting her embroidered apron
picked up the photo frame
    put it down
     picked it up again
asked casually: your sister?
her eyes
evading the issue

2. I turned your photo to the wall
not daring to look you in the face in front of another

As long as the dam holds back the flood
your smile
is the only luxury I allow myself

3. Sentimental geese of the south
daily
rouse a silent tidal wave in my heart

4. Life
History

Even the initial failure to make seedcorn sprout
is an exercise without a solution

5. What is it that is receding, at intervals
a shrill cry in the clouds

What is it that is silently praying, stirring
        my roots under the earth

6. The stream twists and turns
Yaya's train of thought turns and twists
Scrubbing and rubbing she cleans the shirt
of steamy sunlight and greasy soil
Through her womanly tenderness
a generous manly nature
acquires a little purity
        a little uncertainty

Oh, Old Jin's dry pipe
burns the mouth

6. New Year's Eve

1977
she
western Fujian

Three full bowls of rice wine
hot rice dumplings wrapped in bamboo leaves
and then Shanfeng walked with me to the old temple
asking whether I was afraid of keeping watch all alone
  Oh, I'm afraid I'd talk to the cassia tree in the courtyard
   I'm worried I'd listen to the stream's constant murmur
  arousing wind and waves in my heart
  and then the mountains would pile up like dams

I locked and bolted the door
turned up the wick of the oil-lamp to write to you
my head dizzy
my heart throbbing
  Oh, which is the star you walk under
  and do you still remember the magnolia
  Whether you remember or not
  I call out for you so often — why don't you answer

I placed your guitar on my lap
stroked it silently
"Be brave" I told myself
if only to give you peace of mind
    Oh, year after year this endless chase
        yet you are still so far away
        If one day my songs should find you
        will you come, my dear

7. A Cry from Afar

New Year's Eve, 1977
he
north-western China

"my dear, my dear ....
What's that?
Who is it?
    Don't —
I upset the stool
as I opened the window to catch the voice
The clear sky held its breath
The shivering stars sent down their tears —
Is that you
my little murmuring flower
      Where   are   you

What harm have you come to
What is it that transmits
your pain and loneliness
to shatter
my heart and overstrung nerves
Oh
premonitions
dark
like hungry ravens scrambling for food
I opened my arms in vain
Whose but whose
tearful face could I comfort in my embrace

8. *The Lark*

autumn 1978
she
conservatory examination hall

Walking in the biting wind
I feel no sorrow in my heart
Like a lark heralding the coming of spring
I am singing merrily
    (He who grabbed my hand roughly
    I did not back away from him
    My gentleness rested on his feverish forehead
    like a cool tree shade
    like a moistening cloud)

However long the mountain path
it must come to an end
I'm sure the blue sea lies
behind the mountain ranges
    (The lone mouth-organ playing on the far bank
    knew my silent enquiries all too well
    It played another tune, yet another tune
    until a rainy morning unfolded into emblazoned twilight)

I am all alone for now
but loneliness holds no fear for me
There are footprints before me
and I am not the last in the line
        (Whose blurred face was it
        who lit the lamp and chased away the mosquitoes
        whose strong arms carried me
        unconscious, across the mountains
        for forty miles
        who knocked open the proud doors of the mountain clinic
        whose face was blackened by pine knot smoke
        whose name I didn't even know)

Walking in the biting wind
I feel no sorrow in my heart
Like a lark heralding the coming of spring
I am singing merrily
        (All this is why
        I have survived, and will
        never give up singing)

9. Song of Silence

1981
she
after a performance

You
are the constant star
    in my nights of solitude
for ten long and feverish years
the burning sun
brought to maturity my life
    and my emotions
— my dearest

Then the day came
when the sky shattered in flames
In my dizziness
I was welded to centre-stage
between the curtains and the footlights
Who'd have thought
all the birds
my crippled hands had nursed
which had flown away ten years ago
would come back, hover in the air
then land as the sound of applause

To eyes that look like budding leaves
I bow
The stage in my heart
is completely empty

10. After the Election

1983
he
north-western China

Soil
rustling between fingers
like steel files
We know, we know
Oh, there is no need to take an oath
Let the villagers never be hungry
Let the children go to school
That is the plainest of plain truths
That is politics
for a common peasant county head

In the future, there will of course be
orchestras and swimming pools
and a beehive-like
"Trust"

Standing on this new-found peak, perhaps
I will see the ocean I left so long ago
I will see
the red houses burning like a radiant sunset
— Come now, there is no time for this

By then, I'd be an old man
        (this is the first time I have thought of old age)
a tree that grew from your abundance
listening to the talk of a Fourth Wave
telling the children about the land reform

And this must be Yaya coming
her feet you know well
        the past stops her from coming near me
And yet the girl of my memories does not belong
to this land I love passionately

11. *"Would you please give her this note"*

1984
he
National Theatre

In your songs we swim
me
and my son
I am watching the live broadcast
telling my wife to stop husking corn
See, in our county now
we have hot-water bottles and TVs

(I had meant to tell you
about some dreams, off and on
about the warm sun and cold snow of a north-western plateau
about a miracle of telepathy
        that happened on a magnetic night)
Well, I guess not
I don't even want to tell you
how I stood in the rain
for an hour
holding an umbrella to a poster
to stop the rain from teasing
your name in all its finery
Congratulations —

Lamplight is shimmering in the rain
Do forgive this uncouth, faltering hand
    (Oh, a heart that shakes
        a shaking pen)
The unripe fruit of our youth
let it drop unripened
Stop sorrow
    from shading the deep pools of your eyes
I hope your songs
your life
    blossom again like a tree in spring

Urgent Telegram
same night, he, post office
"Yaya, Arriving date
If you agree
we'll marry the same day"

12. *High above the clouds:*
   the loneliness, night after night

same night
she
theatre entrance

Rain
Drizz   ling   down
The lamppost, tired of solitude, sopping wet
bursts into magnolia blooms

A notepaper unfolds
laboriously into a white butterfly
flying unsteadily away
to sink in a puddle

the show is over
....

first draft 1981
final draft 1985

July That Year

1

I see you receding with the quay
back into the July of flaming flowers and twinkling trees
    Which hand
    closes the door for good?
Your July
has just withered

I cannot see your unbending pride
fighting not to drown in the sunset
    The lights glistening along the river
    are all tears, hot tears
My July
is saying farewell

2

I hear your steps meandering along the beach, among
empty stairs, floating crags and hidden rocks
    Will the wind I prayed to
    never blow on your sail?
Life never shed its leaves
in our time of the year

I heard that you climbed the skies
I heard that you have left us far behind
    If this is true, it must be snowing
    all the year round in your heart
Stroking these rumours like piano keys
Your real voice is a field of ashes

3

I imagine your easy manner
handshakes and speeches behind the red table napkin
    Smile rusted onto your face
    Loneliness eaten into your heart
In your blood-vessels the July water
is flickering

The giant hawk on Peak of Edges is not you
You are nowhere in the midnight pines at Windy Pass
    Then for July you are a fantasy
    Then to you July is a blank
I can't imagine how you make yourself believe
by saying — but you've already forgotten

31 January 1985

End of Hibernation

Your beard and long hair are tossing waves
a tangled neglect and disappointment
    no one tends them any more
The past
has retreated into swarthy time
and clustered into woebegone ghost islands
The dazzling sunset on the calm sea
    a moment of tenderness
    a moment of wanness
    a moment's smile like the glittering arc of a wave

You were once paraded through the streets as a dark cloud
with showers of arrows piercing your heart
piercing the hot-blooded pride of your youth
Love picked up in her spotless hand
your shoes trampled by the multitude
put them back on your feet that had to walk on thorns
The angels with their wings
covered your airspace
At that instant
the sharp edge of your sight had risen clear of the mire of fate

But what was the moment
when your soul escaped
your body left behind
the hollow pendulum of your life
like a slow motion shot
    of a precipitous plunge
    down a ravine of dark wind
Your favourite mandolin
scattered plaintive notes all the way
that never after
were set in song

Once you thought you'd sink eternal into the deepest depths
But dawn
broke before time at the gate of hell
The spring rain came late with timid steps
The hesitant light resting on your shoulder span a cobweb
In the sky
countless noises clamoured for attention
The dream of watch-fires and beacons
you had closed your eyes to
broke the dike one spring night racked by the elements
to overflow
into a dark green morning tide

8 March 1985

. . . in between

it's just a common lane
    on the low wall there may be specks
    that may grow in time into a charcoal drawing
perhaps it was a gust of wind
or perhaps a kind of smell
bewilderment sprouts rootlessly

the mind is a compass without direction
    it seems that you've stepped
right into a magnetic field

then you keep trying to recall
    you must have missed something
      what is it that has awaited you for years what is it that you've
        been waiting for

even if you follow your own footprints
you will not return
to where you started

you do not stand up to open the window
one gesture may evoke
countless hints in response
on an ordinary stormy night, recalling
        a pair of wet feet
        a muddy path
what is it that put its paw on your shoulder
in an unguarded moment

it doesn't call, it doesn't answer
it may never have been so close before, but
in a split second, eternity
passes through your nerve network
like wind parting grass and flowering reed

you still cannot tell
where it is or how you feel
a vanishing
        that can never be repeated
and yet so familiar, as if
        you're immersed once again
in the stream of a previous life

3 March 1985

A Letter to the Guitar Girl

A small umbrella
drifting along the lonely long street
drifting in the sad life of a half-breed girl
drifting in my deserted woody hills like mushrooms after rain
then drifting on
        into a Yangtze
        into a Rhine

Don't let your cloudy eyes
soak me through, Renate

The black passion is as hot as drums in the jungle
Fierce horses strum out blue fire on the strings
        A black-haired young mother, with
        a blonde little girl
        enchant me and pain me
Having tuned me into a deep pond of quietude
your fingers are still exploring

What you touch is a wall
It is too late to bring me into the song, Renate

Beside the taxi
in front of the hotel
again we meet and again we say goodbye
Sun and drizzle is the weather of West Berlin
The cheongsam your mother left you wraps your sadness
into a book in Chinese binding
outshining the Gedächtniskirche

We bid our true farewell when we are born
Goodbye, West Berlin; Goodbye Renate!

May 1985

In the Night-club

I don't want to cross the border
With orange juice and beer
as our guards
We each feel so safe
There will be no gunshot
to startle us
    wild ducks
        out on a jaunt
My smiling rushes
bloom on your hazy bank
and sweep low
over the streets of Munich

May 1985

Husum Game Restaurant
— with many stuffed birds on the wall

For all these years
    of beating their wings
        these birds
never managed to fly off
from this wall
        The fire in the hearth
        makes all those wings come alive

He who hides himself in the lamplight
will be frightened by the lamplight
when he sees
    among the distress calls of the birds
    a new sign of desperate struggle
decorating the wall

May 1985

Water Metasequoia

the water feels cold
quietly
it lets the trailing racks of cloud
    bed down into
    cold jade purity

the sunset
contours a mottled musical scale
    that is reaching to the bend of shadowy creek
    fading against the light
    could it be the hand which picks out the notes
autumn turns pale or thick at will
    just like the sky   like the water
each going its way but ravellingly interlinked

that night of insomnia
I tossed, unable to shun your prolonged glance
these last years
I have been trapped on this string every day
every day
on your ambiguous painting
    now awake
        now asleep

till my feet touch the cold
feeling of water
in the warm southern breeze   shuttle
        white butterflies
you call me jasmine   not
knowing
        you were once named water metasequoia
        in a season that died against the light

I won't say
I need not say that I was your kindred spirit
for a moment
that white bright secret ran you through
when I sighed
and suddenly withered   in your hand

7 June 1985

Death of the Monk

longing for the silky fingers
yet hating
        their silky softness
after tasting all the plants
pain has no more shape
you are the solicitous light, the particular smell
        the tonsure
        the motions
        the old fragments
those who pursue you see only your back
turning around: you are a stone statue
your empty sockets stare
over everyone's head

even your nearest and dearest
cannot bear your blinding light
they are like rocks under radiation
eager to crumble to dust
they have no feeling under your tread, since
life
is continuous catastrophe

in order to pour a full cup of yourself
and raise it to the sun
you first plunge into abysmal darkness
        no one can save you
        no hand can reach you
your five senses have long been dead
but the lilt of your laughter
will be heard after centuries
by those ears
attuned to its sound

12 August 1985

The Archaeopteryx

    looking down
on us from the time out of mind

the sky   has no outlines
the jungles the prairies all shadowed by his wings
he is mute among singing birds
the fowls of the air complexly imitate
    his pure and simple silence
ugly   cumbersome   alone
a prey to foes, hunger and exposure
    destroyed in the primeval past
    legendized in the primeval past
his figure as he falls is blotted out
what becomes brighter by and by
    is the background
that dawn of chaos, that primitive sunrise
with a name like the crown
manacled him
to the history of evolution   said to be
the eternal life

with no autobiography   and
no room for thought

November 1985

autumn thoughts

autumn journeys relentlessly on the leaves day and night
the hour strikes
then grows old
and yellow; it
drifts down

we its hostages are swept along
unable to call for help
unwilling to give up the struggle
we hear in our hearts
        chaos   disorder
swarms of wasps in fury
surrounding
a wild haw past its flowering

the path behind us turned cold and dim
we know nothing can be recovered
yet out of habit our eyes linger on the twisting path
the cypress vine has put out small flowers
the roots you have shed
climb up my heart with a piercing pain
every minute you touch turns into the past
before the giant palm
reaches you
think again
you still cannot go home

you may go this way
or that way
at the last we shall meet
autumn makes us full
in the end we shall burst open
like ripened pea-pods

midnight, 21 November 1985

Derailed

A head-on collision at incredible speed
Spectacular annihilation right before our eyes
But
it didn't happen

A door
opened, then shut
That was all
or was it?

Your delayed returning wheels   left
on my barren dream meadow
numerous tracks
to be smoothed out when I wake

February 1986

The Sleeping Clock

— in memoriam

The clock of my yearning
    is forever
    silent
Its notes are like birds flown into the woods
But to you were confided many choruses

The obituary goes up and down
breaking the piggy banks of hearts
and tipping out a hugh heap of stored up sighs
to be all spent at once

Unauthorized, the fingers of remembrance
reach into your past and feel around
They may find pieces of a broken spring
Assembled with care
could it be that clock

The man looks paler inside the black frame
The flame tree stands outside the window
    bright red
    in the rain

Summer 1986

where the soul dwells

all roads lead to you
none of them reach you

your words are compiled into dictionaries
those who keep copies of your silence
have their own renditions in their hearts

you locked the door
then threw away the key
you never walk down that street, yet each time
you look up you see a window open

catcalls and applause
sedimentary rocks are soft
before they turn into amber
    amid the lush foliage
that cicada of yours

shrills

1986

That Primary Colour

back again to the river
    the yellow river
hammer it straight
pump it dry
stretch it till its joints crack and seethe
    and then
        let it explode into thin air

the golden headband of beads
describe an arc
        from east to west
                of flame and fluorescence
the awe of the multitudes

a moment of splendour
a long life of pain

who can fly eternally in the sky
who can leap like a tamed lion
        through the row of years
        with every day a burning hoop
millions of hands reach to the magnificent sea
        to salvage the sinking sun
while from the black soil
seeds of fire
are sprouting silently

you may conquer the sky once again
but in the end
you return to the trampled earth

15 August 1986

"forget-me-not"

a blue flame
leaping between icy currents of printed words
a pocket-book drops from my hand
before it reaches the floor
I have accomplished
a beautiful elopement

can I say it's you
simply you?
    unforeseen meetings in the future
    indexed entries in my diaries
    a long letter
    a signed blank page
or a birthday blossom kept fresh in the wrappings of memory
stretching its tendrils from our youth into the present

I remember
it's been hundreds of years
for hundreds of years
the soul sloughs off its exuviae
why should it be awakened
by these three burning words

forget me not
forget me not
who has forgotten me
whom did I forget

17 July 1986

goodbye, white handkerchief

under a gold-plated number on such-and-such a door
on such-and-such a street in such-and-such a city
a man took out a neatly folded handkerchief
gave it to a young woman to dress her wounded ankle
she turned him down
ever since then they said they didn't know
what street or what city or what door it was
the handkerchief sat white and elegant
at an angle in the man's jacket
on rainy days sunny days
no-rain-no-sun days
the girl's wound continued to smart

countless days countless months and countless years passed
the man's and the woman's emotions underwent
a great many seasonal changes
they met behind another door
not the one on that street in that city
he was not a man just a briefcase
she not a woman just some documents
gently they greeted each other
gently they bade each other goodbye
gently they rubbed their noses
the white handkerchief looked embarrassed
the red bloodstain shifted quietly to her heart

for all the bird tongues they knew they could not communicate
instead they folded their names into small soaring kites
longing to be read
"however round a circle you draw it's not art
if you're not in it"
with every "flat" the man drew on his documents
he broke a pen
"But where can I find you again?"
the woman crossed out a number in her phone book
it's said she didn't cry

6 June 1986

a night at an inn

traces of lipstick and tears
join forces in an ad for love
that bravely climbs into a postal box
a cold postal box
long disused
its seal drifts like a bandage in the wind

eaves undulate softness under the black cat's claws
sleep is pressed thin and hard by container trucks
the sprinter
dreams all night of the starting shot
a magician drops his eggs
street lamps scream as they explode
splashing egg-yolk on the night
emaciated night

a night-gowned woman
flings open the door with world-shattering noise
darts along the carpet like a deer
a huge moth skirting the wall
rushes into the flames of the ringing phone

the receiver holds
silence
only snow
keeps singing in distant telephone lines

30 November 1986 in Fuzhou

Mirror

The dark blue night
old wounds break open all at once
As it cooks and bakes the past
the bed is an infinitely patient lover
The tick-tock tick-tock of the clock
tramples your dreams beyond salvation
Groping along the wall
groping for the pull-switch
you entangle unwittingly
a skein of moonlight
At the smell the silver fish swarm up the stem
and you become
limp like a pool of water

As you slowly turn over
　　　　you look at yourself
　　　　you look at yourself

The dressing mirror pretends to a blameless devotion
The sordid wallpaper blurs its pattern
Rigidly framed
you watch yourself shed one petal after another
        there is no escape no escape
Even if you could jump back over one wall after another
the impassable days behind you will block your retreat
Women need no philosophy
Women can shake off the spots on the moon
like dogs shake off water

Draw the thick curtain
dawn has its wet tongue on the window pane
Return to the hollow of the pillow
let yourself unwind
like a roll of exposed film

The walnut tree at the window shudders noisily
as if touched by a cold hand

1986-1987

Waters of Green Lake
— on the road from Huian to Chongwu Highway

green is the water of the lake
one kiss
and the face is marked with the colour of moss
pain finally surfaced from the depth of the heart
surfaced as a memorial
her navy-topped black-trousered friends standing in a circle
their sadness forgotten
they brush their floral kerchiefs and look
towards the clear autumn sky
cascading over their heads
like icy water

gently curved eyebrows
painting an ancient rule into beauty and charm
discoloured fingers curl into a question mark
the earth holds no regrets
but the trees lament
the wind softly puts down a few yellow leaves
thirty-five years in a flash
her half-open eyes are now free of sorrow
free of sorrow the sunlight
leaps and bounces through the crowd

Editor's Note: This is one of two poems Shu Ting has written about Huian minority women, the other (and better-known) poem being "Women of Huian" 惠安女子. "Waters of Green Lake" is based on the suicide of a local woman. As mentioned in stanza four, suicide was common among these women oppressed by poverty and traditional values, and some of the deaths are immortalized in folklore. Suicide Cliff and Women's Pool are two of the local places favoured by Huian women who want to take their own lives.

her ten-year-old daughter changes her clothes with shaking
    hands
her eight-year-old daughter wails on someone's lap
the four-year-old
crawls along the gutter pulling up clumps of daisies
a local writer passing through pats her head
"Mama has just gone to sleep"

other babies in the village are all betrothed soon after birth
at seven or eight months an unbetrothed girl
is an old maid is left-over goods
the women of Huian wear no glass slippers
their earliest education is Suicide Cliff and Women's Pool
it's too late
to tell her the events of a decade later
her daughters may become engineers, managers, or mayors
to a mother
the most secure prospect of all
is that of a bride

the path she inherited
that curled in her bosom like a cobra
unfurled and lay under her feet
enticing her to jump
life is so hard
but is death any easier
her mouth is still half-open
is the legacy for three future young mothers
a floral kerchief
a silver belt   a bracelet
and a lake of green water

the spectators crowded together and then dispersed
two teenage girls sporting bamboo hats
are asked to be photographed
by some travel magazine
there is a serious debate
over whether they should wipe away their tears
the girls walked away slowly along the lake shore
where the water
bites into their trouser hems
and then tears to shreds
their graceful figures

29 November 1987

sunset on White Creeper Lake

far away, beyond my reach
there you are
a spark of fire behind a snow curtain
pushed slowly closer by the sunset, turning into
a pair of warm eyes
ripples all over the lake
break into a smile

at the water's edge bark cabins line the village
broad, soft plantain leaves
  see you off mile after mile
a little blue bird rests on the reed
puzzled by the solemn silence
  its questioning notes of surprise
disappear into the lake
you are the sinking bell
growing into a tree of flame on the other side
but you are no longer ours

red clouds surge into the sky
everyone tinted by the glow is
a music fountain
pushed by joy and sorrow
to a heart-rending climax

in the resonance of the rippling lake
I shake like a leaf
let tears cover my face
the feast of youth has no place for me
what must I do to find the way
that will lead me
to completion

16 January 1988 at the White Creeper Lake Resort

Curriculum Vitae

My mother
tossed and turned in her marble urn
crystallizing all my dreams of her
into icicles
We brothers and sisters pooled together some money
Mother moved to a graveyard with a lawn and chirring insects
The south drizzles on the "Zhangzhou white" tombstone
drizzles on Mother's name
We stood in rows
exceptionally white and dazzling

Grandma and Grandpa have long been crushed and flattened
under a newly constructed brewery, their
many children scattered around the country all prosperous
like beer froth
overflowing into a drizzling Qingming morning
this must be a site of excellent *fengshui*
the photo of Grandpa and Grandma stands amongst Auntie's
    antique furniture
innocent and at ease

Editor's Note: White is the colour of mourning in China. Qingming is the family grave-sweeping day in the third month of the lunar year (usually in April). The grand- and great-grandparents in this poem are on Shu Ting's maternal side, in whose house she grew up. Usual Chinese practice traces one's lineage on the paternal rather than the maternal side. This poem is a reflection of the heavy influence Shu Ting's early life and her maternal family had on her.

Great-grandpa's soul is a homeless wanderer
following the place-of-birth column to the old Zhangzhou plains
his pedlar's basket lost forever
he can only blow his nose noisily
        (Grandma said he suffered from sinusitis)
his myopic eyes scrutinizing every door in every home
his red nose shaped like a snail
sticking to other families' window panes

the rain has stopped
a huge shadow on the wall snatches at me
I bend down to open the bookcase
and am caught by my own shadow
the pale halo of the wall lamp is a warm consolation
I will accept
the strange attention
from eons ago and eons to be
a vague shape in the darkness — that's me

January 1988

A Letter to Second Uncle

Second Uncle lives in Taipei
Taipei is a street with sheltered walkways
When it rains in Xiamen
that street gets wet too — the wetness
on Uncle's bushy eyebrows
When the magnolia blooms on that street
fragrance fills the Xiamen old home on Palace Road
fragrance fills a tin of old yellowed photographs
photographs of Second Uncle with a crew cut
glancing sideways mischievously
Ah
Old Grandpa's fingers shake, sifting through the photos

Second Uncle crossed the sea to pursue his studies
taking with him a handful of soil, a bottle of water
a plain savoury cake, a green olive
Fourth Uncle's New Year pocket money
First Auntie's carefully stitched quilt
and
        how did you see them without looking back
Grandma's silent tears

Second Uncle left with his head held high
his pockets stuffed with all the snacks he loved
little knowing
this street and that street
both with sheltered walkways, would remain
disconnected for forty-five years

And then under the loquat tree
you sent your daughter off to study in Japan
          this time the one with her head held high
          was my delighted little cousin
You finally learnt how Grandma's nightly prayers
were rejected by the stars and the waves
The dream no longer whole
a half moon shines on either side

The older the papaya tree, the sweeter the fruit
This one is still scarred with your childhood
practice of spear routines
The older Grandma was, the deeper her longing
In moments of confusion she told us to buy frosted candy, to buy
the preserved plums Little Chang loved so much
When she was even older she lay in bed
counting the number of Taiwan visitors walking past our door
"Why don't I hear your Second Uncle's footsteps
he always wears his shoes back to front"

March 1989

The Time of Power Failure

> *Writing poetry is instinct*
> *being called a poet is pure chance*
>
> — *Shu Ting*

The evening with no light
is a mud-flat
People
ordered into exile by their strange homes
straggle on a lawn
in twos and threes

Projecting themselves on panicky voices
they seem to be guarding
empty fortresses
Time and again they trip over
meaningless conversation

In the building nearby
spiky candle flames, guarded by hands
move
from one window
to another window
Black tides lap up and eddy away
Many eyes
are bright this moment
dark the next

Something begins to stir
scorches the breast
is it that thing called thought
The handle is grasped
The rusted door squeaks
the soul is eager to break away

Your wife calls
Your kids take out their homework
The singer singing on TV sees you and smiles
Dreams and last night's fallen hair are left on the pillow
moored
on the deep ponds and shallow streams of lamps
The fish are quiet
Some windows are blue
Some windows are gold
Ali Baba, Ali Baba
Is there really a secret door

13 March 1989

A Style of Playing

The trumpet is the lamplight from a lone house in the wilderness
the saxophone is soft gentle snow
  falling
layer upon layer
The trumpet shimmers in the thin haze
in the saxophone's pond
  croaking frogs tense up and slacken
  leaves of grass bend under the weight of fireflies
The trumpet is a tallow tree in autumn
the saxophone, torn up in the whirlwind, dances
its last dance around the arms of the praying tree
  the ground is stained red

The trumpet soars suddenly
the saxophone, with misty toes, with forest sounds, with deer
  horns
    climbs up slowly
      step by step
The trumpet leaps out
the saxophone stretches into an expanse of ocean
  wave after wave
  sunlight the colour of metal
The trumpet has victory in its grasp
the saxophone calls forth its army of thousands
The trumpet launches an all out attack
the saxophone
oh the saxophone suddenly drops to a murmur

The trumpet throws itself down the abyss
breaking into echoes of raindrops and scattering pearls
the saxophone stands howling on the stone ridge
carrying on its back the huge sinking sun

Fuzhou, 9 May 1990

Reading at Night

The most charming most alive of Chinese words
free themselves from book bindings
like gorgeously-coloured birds
spreading their wings gracefully
to reveal the mixed forest where they rest

They choose their own companions
extending a limited journey into eternity
giving music to the voiceless
endowing the voiceless with form

It is impossible to make them stay
to harm them only brings self-humiliation
they come at will
they leave at will
Brushed by their soft feathery wings
my blank manuscript paper
stays
azure like clear sky after rain

10 May 1990

The age of autumn

who has detected the first whiff of autumn
in the south, autumn holds no fear for the leaves
pigeons occupy the meat market and the skies
the sorrowful geese
flying in formation as a short poem or a long verse
only cry about the chill in ancient texts
florists display chrysanthemums and butterfly grass
seasonal expressions replicated in greenhouses
are as good as real

autumn invades perhaps at noon perhaps at dawn perhaps
when you find the cicadas have effected a total retreat
the woods are still
in their concealed attention
the old banyan tree still sweeps the ground
the woman with her hair in a chignon walks carefully down the
        steps
a little pitiful because
the sunlight turns suddenly
into a tired glance

quenching in the furnace of summer
has not purified my heart of all its sand
though it now shines brilliantly like a dagger
too dangerous to give to another
for fear of hurting myself
a heart drumming thunderously
a face like an old temple grown with moss

no need to check the calendar
for me autumn came eight years ago

5 September 1990

Afterword: Some Thoughts on Shu Ting's Poetry
By Chen Zhongyi

Artists and poets are sometimes divided into two broad catego-
ries: the extrovert and the introvert. The former are usually inspired
by the objective world; all subject-matter, provided it has "caught" the
artist's "eye of wisdom", can easily fuel his creative furnace. A cinematic
analogy: the extroverts are character actors, equally at home in portray-
ing a child's naïveté or an old man's obstinacy, a man's aggressiveness
or a woman's tenderness. The introverts are just the opposite. The
journey of the heart and soul is at the centre of their creation: every-
thing revolves around personal experience. However significant an
event, however great a miracle, if it does not touch their innate
sensitivity or stimulate their deeply hidden "points of contact", it will
fail to inspire no matter how favourable the conditions for creation. It
is as if they concentrate their attention on a well, staring fixedly at the
thread of water running from its source. They do not aspire to the
breadth of lakes and seas, but concentrate only on plumbing the depths
of this well.

Shu Ting is an introvert poet. Extrovert poets subject their senses
to all dimensions, and are forever ready to embrace the world and to
capture every transient "moment" of inspiration. Shu Ting, however,
becomes "engulfed" by the world of ordinary "onlookers" and, as an
ordinary woman with ordinary vision and feelings, dissolves herself in
life, becoming a mere bubble in its stream, a bit of straw, a fallen leaf.
It is evident that she blocks off her senses, and does not incite or
stimulate them. Instead, she instinctively lets them either flourish or
wither. She does not embrace the objective world wholeheartedly. Only
when a certain "moment" touches the right chord in her heart can her
state of mind possibly become that of a poet.

Shu Ting has been labelled a poet for quite some time, but her actual time spent writing poetry amounts to no more than a hundred-odd hours. And she has only written a hundred-odd poems over the past twenty years, averaging less than ten per year. (She has even been known to stop writing altogether for two or three years at a time.) She has never written a single pure landscape poem even though she has travelled half of China, and she maintained a long silence following encounters with exotic cultures on trips to Europe, India and America. Even today, she laments the "great misconception" of her as a poet.

She has such a careless, casual attitude towards poetry that she is wont to neglect her own career as a professional writer. She is more like a carefree child forever playing truant, who looks upon homework as an imposition. She prefers to ramble along the coast, picking up the odd shell whenever the mood takes her. When poets hold fast to their "sensitivity zones", what they express is far from shallow. But the various mysteries of a boundless universe are ignored.

Shu Ting's main concern is with human relations. Perhaps deep childhood impressions of friendship and hardship are more readily absorbed by her "inspirational spectrum". We discover that her initial points of reference are always definite and concrete. Shu Ting herself once said that every one of her poems is written to a particular person. But as a result of the collective psychological trauma experienced during a particular period of history, a poem written to an individual can attain the breadth of feeling of a whole generation. In this way Shu Ting transcends herself. Perhaps it is fair to say that, while her creative state of mind is constantly introverted, the effect is not infrequently extrovert; she seems to tread the brink between the two.

The apathy and estrangement caused by the ten-year Cultural Revolution touched her kind and pacifist nature, and she responded instantly and instinctively. Through poems of farewell, poems to a distant friend, poems of nostalgia, she articulates what she sees as expiring humanity and love. In those ten years she was depressed, confused and alone. But she was steadfast and patient in the pursuit of her ideals. The bittersweetness of this pursuit involved trust,

reconciliation, respect and compassion, and has inspired the compo-
sition of a concerto of universal love.

In 1980, Shu Ting was beginning to be understood, and readers
found it easier to identify with her than with other poets of the *Today*
group: firstly, her romantic lyrical quality is tinged with classical charm
and restrained elegance, attracting those contemporary readers
trained in classical poetry. There is tremendous variety in her expres-
sion and her technique marks the beginning of a depolarization of
tradition and modernism. Secondly, she emerged at a time when new
poetry was in a state of fragmentation. In an expanse of wasteland, just
one or two flowers are enough to dazzle: favourable conditions made
her famous for a time. But more importantly, she always sailed the
borderline between the familiar and the unfamiliar within the reader's
field of vision. Her popularity stemmed from an understanding of the
world which coincided with the receptive focus of the majority of her
readers. But the aesthetic of society changes rapidly as does the cycle
of artistic development. It is increasingly obvious that the ever-so-pop-
ular Shu Ting is being re-evaluated in the context of such changes.

Years ago, there was heated debate in poetry circles over the
political tendency of Shu Ting's poems. Her supporters referred to her
as "the progressive among the passive"; her critics described her as "the
stirred-up dregs of the Crescent Moon School" [of the 1920s], "a
straggler unworthy of mention". Now that people are no longer at
loggerheads with each other over such irrelevant questions, the rich-
ness of her feelings in their sincerity and dignity is becoming generally
acknowledged.

Since 1980, I have discussed Shu Ting's poems both in public and
in private, and protested at the description of them as "stirred-up dregs
of the twenties and thirties" —this vulgar sociological approach stifles
the polyphony and variation in her poems. But this is not to say that
I agree with those radicals who look upon her as the vanguard of
the modernist school —she is not a bridge to the future, rather, she
echoes a transition from the romantic towards the modernistic. The

philosophy of the mean, so deeply rooted in the Chinese mind, is something of an obstacle to the re-orientation demanded by rapid change. Shu Ting has succeeded in adjusting the sights of her readers by "welding" the modern to the traditional.

If "The Singing Iris" (1981) is the watershed between her pure romantic style and her syncretism, the poem "The Archaeopteryx" (1985) verges on the modernistic and signals a departure from her singularly emotional approach: the expression in her earlier work, characterized by simplicity, has become deeper and denser. Shu Ting's admiration for human sincerity had initially galvanized her creativity but "The Archaeopteryx" indicated a fresh fascination with the mysteries of life. Ideals and humanity began to recede.

Having gained insight into the positive side of humankind, Shu Ting cast a perplexed eye over the negative side. Consciously or not, she began to bore through the outer layers of human sincerity in order to examine the unfathomable "black box". Deep within, her emotional experiences undoubtedly began to give way to a more ontological perspective. Personal emotional inspiration has been supplanted by a deeper understanding of human existence which has undeniably broadened her perception of the world. One might say that she is walking slowly through the gates of modernism. But, it seems to me, she does so somewhat unconsciously in that it is a classical and romantic heritage which dominates her creative being.

Translated by Oliver Stunt & Chu Chiyu

Translators

Eva Hung translated To an Oak, Longing, A roadside encounter, Assembly Line, Homeward bound, A Love Song for this Land, Brother, I'm here, In Memory of My Late Grandmother, Twelve Nights of the Milky Way (TV Poetry), ... in between, Autumn thoughts, Derailed, Where the soul dwells, "Forget-me-not", Goodbye, white handkerchief, A night at an inn, Waters of Green Lake, Sunset on White Creeper Lake, Curriculum Vitae, A Letter to Second Uncle, A Style of Playing, Reading at Night and The age of autumn.

Tao Tao Liu translated Gifts, A Boat with Two Masts, Goodbye in the Rain and A Boat.

Gordon Osing & De-an Wu Swihart translated When You Walk Beneath My Window, Two, Maybe Three Different Memories, Perhaps and Fallen Leaf.

Janice Wickeri translated The Singing Iris.

Henry Y.H. Zhao & D.E. Pollard translated A Late Autumn Evening in Beijing, Evening Star, Evening Montage, Ah Min in the Café, Resurrection, July That Year, End of Hibernation, A Letter to the Guitar Girl, In the Night-club, Husum Game Restaurant, Water Metasequoia, Death of the Monk, The Archaeopteryx, The Sleeping Clock, That Primary Colour, Mirror and The Time of Power Failure.

Renditions Paperbacks

CURRENT TITLES:

GU CHENG: *Selected Poems*
ISBN 962-7255-05-X

HAN SHAOGONG: *Homecoming and Other Stories*
ISBN 962-7255-13-0

DAVID HAWKES: *A Little Primer of Tu Fu*
ISBN 962-7255-02-5

LI YU: Silent Operas
ISBN 962-7255-07-6

LIU SOLA: *Blue Sky Green Sea and Other Stories*
ISBN 962-7255-12-2

LIU XINWU: *Black Walls and Other Stories*
ISBN 962-7255-06-8

MO YAN: *Explosions and Other Stories*
ISBN 962-7255-10-5

TAO YANG: *Borrowed Tongue*
ISBN 962-201-381-3

WANG ANYI: *Love in a Small Town*
ISBN 962-7255-03-3

WANG ANYI: *Love on a Barren Mountain*
ISBN 962-7255-09-2

XI XI: *My City: a hongkong story*
ISBN 962-7255-11-4

XI XI: *A Girl Like Me and Other Stories*
ISBN 962-201-382-1

YU LUOJIN: *A Chinese Winter's Tale*
ISBN 962-201-383-X

A Golden Treasury of Chinese Poetry
ISBN 962-7255-04-1

Contemporary Women Writers: Hong Kong and Taiwan
ISBN 962-7255-08-4

Orders and enquiries to:
Renditions, Chinese University of Hong Kong, Shatin, NT., Hong Kong
Telephone (852) 2609-7407   Fax (852) 2603-5149